The Living World of Marsupials

Written by Madeline Tyler
Designed by Daniel Scase

BookLife PUBLISHING

©Published 2022.
BookLife Publishing Ltd.
King's Lynn, Norfolk PE30 4LS

ISBN 978-1-80155-157-1

All rights reserved. Printed in Poland.
A catalogue record for this book is available
from the British Library.

The Lives of Marsupials
Written by Madeline Tyler. Adapted by William Anthony
Designed by Daniel Scase

An Introduction to Accessible Readers…

Our 'really readable' Accessible Readers have been specifically created to support the reading development of young readers with learning differences, such as dyslexia.

Our aim is to share our love of books with children, providing the same learning and developmental opportunities to every child.

INCREASED FONT SIZE AND SPACING improves readability and ensures text feels much less crowded.

OFF-WHITE BACKGROUNDS ON MATTE PAPER improves text contrast and avoids dazzling readers.

SIMPLIFIED PAGE LAYOUT reduces distractions and aids concentration.

CAREFULLY CRAFTED along guidelines set out in the British Dyslexia Association's Dyslexia-Friendly Style Guide.

Additional images courtesy of Shutterstock.com. 4-5 – Alberto Gomez Pando Baena, Andrii Slonchak. 6-7 – EA Given, Chris Howey. 8-9 – Susan Flashman, imagevixen. 10-11 – Ecopix, Anom Harya. 12-13 – rickyd, TM picture. 14-15 – Susan Flashman, Susan Flashman. 16-17 – Arnaud Martinez, slowmotiongli. 18-19 – Richard A Wall, Chris de Blank. 20-21 – Phillip Minnis, Maik Boenig. 22-23 – Marko Bowman, BMJ. 24-25 – imagevixen, LCAT Productions. 26-27 – Phillip W. Kirkland, Manon van Os. 28-29 – Martin Pelanek, Mandy Creighton.

Contents

Page 4   What Is a Marsupial?

Page 6   Body Parts

Page 12   Moving Around

Page 14   Eating

Page 16   Habitats

Page 20   Adaptation

Page 22   Life Cycle

Page 26   Amazing Marsupials

Page 30   Index

Page 32   The Lives of Marsupials: Quiz

What Is a Marsupial?

Marsupials are warm-blooded mammals that produce milk for their young. Most marsupials have a pouch. Young marsupials live in the pouch until they are big enough to explore outside. Lots of marsupials live in Australia.

There are over 300 types of marsupial. Although marsupials are similar to each other, they are all suited to living in different places. Some marsupials live in trees and others live in burrows under ground.

Body Parts

Marsupials come in all shapes and sizes. They can sometimes look quite different from each other. Most marsupials are born very early and feed on their mother's milk from inside the pouch.

Many marsupials have long, strong tails. Some marsupials, such as kangaroos and wallabies, use their tails for balance as they jump. They can also use them to push themselves forward, like a fifth leg. The tail is so strong that it can hold the kangaroo's body weight.

Nearly all female marsupials have a pouch. The pouch is a fold of skin that covers the mother's teats. When a new baby is born, it crawls through its mother's fur into her pouch.

A newborn marsupial is very small when it first enters the mother's pouch. It stays safe and warm in the mother's pouch for around eight months. When it is big and strong enough, it leaves the pouch for good.

Some marsupials live high up in the forest trees. They must travel from tree to tree to find food and escape from predators. Some trees are very far apart, so certain marsupials have special bits of skin called patagia.

The patagia act like wings and allow the animals to glide from tree to tree. There are seven types of gliding possum that use patagia to do this.

Moving Around

Marsupials move around in different ways depending on where they live.

Marsupials that only live in trees are called arboreal marsupials. They are very good at holding onto tree branches.

Marsupials that live on the land are called terrestrial marsupials. Some terrestrial marsupials use four legs to move across the ground.

Kangaroos have two legs and two arms. They jump forwards by using both feet at the same time.

Eating

Marsupials all have different teeth depending on whether they eat other animals, plants or both.

Tasmanian devils eat mostly animals. They also eat animals that have already died, called carrion. Tasmanian devils have long, sharp teeth to tear meat easily.

The tiger quoll hunts small animals such as birds, rats, possums and rabbits. Tiger quolls are also scavengers. This means that they eat the meat of animals that other predators have already killed.

Habitats

Habitats are the homes of living things. They provide food and shelter for the plants and animals that live in them.

There are a lot of places for a marsupial to live.

Kangaroos live on grasslands, while marsupial moles burrow under ground. Marsupial mice live on the forest floor and gliding possums live high up in the trees.

The koala's favourite food is eucalyptus leaves. They spend all of their time eating and sleeping, so they sit in eucalyptus trees where they can reach their food and stay safe from hungry animals on the ground.

Koalas are strong and have sharp claws on their feet. This helps them to grip onto tree branches so that they don't fall off.

Koalas can eat up to one kilogram of eucalyptus leaves and sleep for 18 hours every day!

Adaptation

Adaptations are changes that help an animal to survive. Many marsupials have adapted to their habitats.

Water opossums live in streams and lakes. Their fur is short so that it doesn't soak up water. They also have webbed feet to help them swim.

Wombats are very good diggers. When they are digging their burrows, they shovel soil towards their bodies. Wombats have backwards pouches that open at the bottom to stops soil from getting inside their pouch. What a special adaptation!

Life Cycle

The life cycle of an animal is the changes it goes through from the start to the end of its life. The life cycle of marsupials is similar to mammals.

Let's look at the life cycle of a kangaroo.

A baby marsupial is called a joey. Joeys are born after just a few weeks. Newborn joeys are pink, very small, hairless, blind and have no ears.

They grow inside their mother's pouch, where they feed on milk.

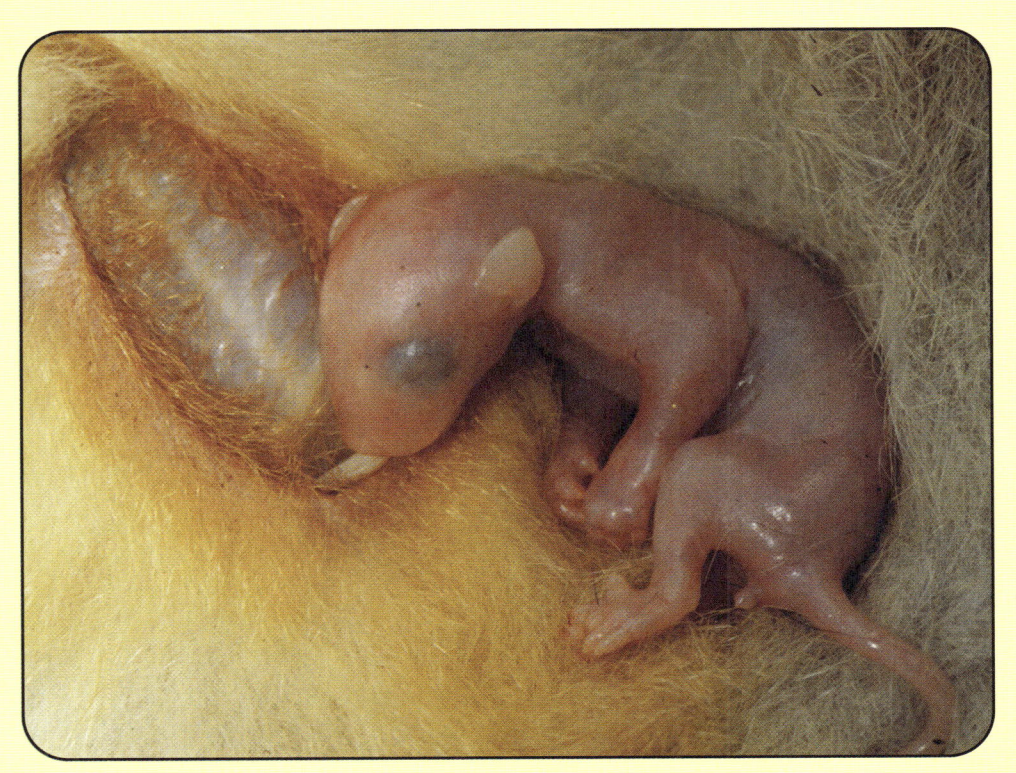

When it is around eight months old, the joey is too big for the pouch. It has grown a lot and can now explore further. However, it will still return to the pouch to drink its mother's milk.

Kangaroos become adults when they are around two years old. They are now big and old enough to have joeys of their own.

Female joeys stay with their mothers. Male joeys leave to find a group of their own.

Amazing Marsupials

Venomous snakes kill their prey by biting and injecting them with something harmful called venom. Virginia opossums are immune to snake venom. This means that they will not be harmed if they are bitten by a snake.

Koalas are one of the few animals that can eat eucalyptus leaves. These leaves can make lots of animals feel unwell because they are very poisonous. However, the koala's body can break down the leaves.

Wombats, like many other animals, are territorial. This means that they have their own area that they guard against other animals. Territorial animals mark their area with their smell to let other animals know that it is taken.

Wombats do this by leaving poo on top of rocks and logs around their area! This means other wombats can easily find it. They have cube-shaped poo that can easily balance and not roll away.

Index:

food 4, 6, 10, 14–16, 18–19, 23–24, 27

habitats 5, 10–13, 16–21

joeys 4, 23–25

patagia 10–11

pouches 4, 6, 8–9, 21, 23

tails 7

The Lives of Marsupials: Quiz

1. What is a baby marsupial called?

2. Where do sugar gliders live?

    (a) In trees
    (b) On the ground
    (c) In lakes and streams

3. What is the favourite food of the koala?

4. Can you use the index page to find information about tails?

5. If you had a zoo and could only look after one marsupial, which one would you choose? Why?

Helpful Hints for Reading at Home

This 'really readable' Accessible Reader has been carefully written and designed to help children with learning differences whether they are reading in the classroom or at home. However, there are some extra ways in which you can help your child at home.

- Try to provide a quiet space for your child to read, with as few distractions as possible.

- Try to allow your child as much time as they need to decode the letters and words on the page.

- Reading with a learning difference can be frustrating and difficult. Try to let your child take short, managed breaks between reading sessions if they begin to feel frustrated.

- Build your child's confidence with positive praise and encouragement throughout.

- Your child's teacher, as well as many charities, can provide you with lots of tips and techniques to help your child read at home.